Money for Beginners

L. RANDALL WRAY

Illustrated by Heske van Doornen

MONEY

FOR BEGINNERS

Polity

First published in 2023 by Polity Press

Polity Press
65 Bridge Street
Cambridge CB2 1UR, UK

Polity Press
111 River Street
Hoboken, NJ 07030, USA

ISBN-13: 978-1-5095-5460-7
ISBN-13: 978-1-5095-5461-4 (pb)

A catalogue record for this book is available from the British Library.

Library of Congress Control Number: 2022946154

Typeset in 12 on 14.5pt Adobe Caslon
by Cheshire Typesetting Ltd, Cuddington, Cheshire
Printed and bound in Great Britain by TJ Books Ltd, Padstow, Cornwall

For further information on Polity, visit our website:
politybooks.com

Contents

Introduction

Money makes the world go 'round, but thinking about it can be overwhelming. You probably sense that almost every issue starts and ends with money. Too much, too little, too cheap, too dear. It is hard to get your mind around the topic of money. You use it every day, but you may not feel as if you really know much about it. Where does it come from? Is Uncle Sam going to run out? Are *you* going to run out? What the heck *is* money, anyway? It is a mystery.

This book will help you to answer those questions for yourself. What you're going to find after reading this book is that money isn't so complicated *after all*. You'll see how both banks and the government create money. You'll understand the relation between government spending and taxation. You'll be able to identify the true constraints we face in trying to tackle our nation's problems and which ones are bogus.

After reading this book, you'll know more about money than most politicians do. That's a **guarantee**. They won't be able to bamboozle you anymore. You'll easily spot their mistakes. The most common error is to confuse the finances of a household with the finances of our nation's government. After reading this book you will understand that Uncle Sam's budget is different from ours: he can't run out of money. And that is a good thing! He can always afford to help us when we need it.

You will also understand what money is, where it comes from, and how banks operate. You will know how our nation's central bank – the Federal Reserve – works with both private banks and the US Treasury to keep our financial system safe. Most importantly, your understanding of money will help prepare you to tackle the challenges we face in coming years.

One of the biggest stumbling blocks to reform is the question: "How are you going to pay for it?" Where will Uncle Sam find the money to repair the nation's infrastructure? To move to sustainable energy? To pay for Social Security's retirees? To reduce unemployment and poverty? To prepare students for our rapidly changing world?

After reading this book, you will have an answer to the "pay for" question.

The purpose of this book is not to take on those policy issues themselves but, rather, to build an understanding of how we can use our financial system to tackle today's problems as well as those of the future.

One final note: we have purposely kept this book short, simple, and uncomplicated by leaving out footnotes and references. For those who want more details, including references for the arguments made, please see the companion volume: *Making Money Work for Us: How MMT Can Transform America*, by L. Randall Wray (Cambridge: Polity, 2022).

1
Money: An Introduction

Money is a complex topic. It is fascinating. It is scary. We'll make it a bit less complicated.

Let's begin with the story of money: What can you do with it, what is it, and where does it come from? You probably use it every day, so that's a good place to start.

Someone hands you some cash. What are you going to do with it?

You can save it! To buy a house. To go to college. For retirement.

More likely, you'll spend it – at least, most of it. We need

PUT IT IN YOUR PIGGY BANK

money to keep us adequately fed, clothed, and sheltered. We work so that we can get paid in money and purchase many of the necessities of life. Except for those at the tippy-top of the income distribution, we spend most of the money we receive.

YOU CAN SPEND IT!

LIVE THE LIFE OF RILEY

Of course, you can run out of it. Spend too much and you are called a *spendthrift*. Strangely, a spendthrift is the opposite of one who is thrifty: spendthrifts spend themselves into poverty. That is, without money.

Save too much, and you are a Scrooge – despised as a miser who hates Christmas.

It is hard to find the right balance between thrifty and spendthrifty!

Carried to the extreme, hoarding money is recognized as a neurosis.

The miser who cannot part with his gold coins is like the baby holding on to feces: according to Sigmund Freud, those who hoard money are the same type who hoarded their poop as babies.

YOU CAN PSYCHOANALYZE IT!

But, of course, we need money. John Maynard Keynes, the father of *macroeconomics*, says it provides us with the means to live wisely, agreeably, and well. But he likens the love of money to a semi-criminal and pathological neurosis.

MONEY MAKES THE WORLD GO 'ROUND.

HOUSEHOLDS SPEND IT

BANKS STORE IT

STORES ACCEPT IT

...AND UNCLE SAM TAKES IT AWAY FROM US IN TAXES.

Businesses borrow money from banks to hire workers and pay them wages. Workers deposit their wages in banks and gradually draw down deposits as they pay bills and buy groceries.

Sales by businesses move those deposits to their own accounts, allowing them to pay down their loans from the banks.

Today, more and more of those transactions take place electronically – through "keystrokes" on computers.

Some say we'll soon have nothing but "digital money." For many, that is perplexing. How can we get by without money that we can touch, put in our pocket, and toss into the air to choose whether to kick or receive the football?

What the heck is a virtual currency that doesn't exist? Is Bitcoin money, and is it our future?

Money can be scary. When I wrote my 1998 book, titled *Understanding Modern Money*, I was warned that "It will scare the heck out of everybody." They were right. It did.

IT STILL DOES.
TWENTY-FIVE YEARS LATER.

MONEY

Let's try to make it a bit less frightening.

In the next chapter we'll investigate money's "genesis" – that is, its origins story – to see if that sheds light on its "nature," just as the Bible's Genesis shed light on the nature of humankind's "original sin."

2
Money: An Origins Story

Let's take a look at what we use today: metal coins, paper bills, checks, plastic cards, and digital transactions. Quite a variety! What do they all have in common? They keep track of something.

And that something is ... *Debt*.

Money began with people trying to keep track of how much they owed someone else.

CURRENCY IS THE IOU OF UNCLE SAM

Let's begin with cash – paper notes (currency) and coins. You know that the paper dollar is green, with George Washington on the front, signed by the US Treasurer and the Secretary of the Treasury.

On the back it says IN GOD WE TRUST, with a picture of an eye on top of a pyramid, as well as some Latin words. That's a bit strange. On further inspection, you'll notice it says "This note is legal tender for all debts, public and private." Whatever that means! (We'll see later.)

The quarter also has a picture of dear old George, also trusts in God, and has an eagle or a symbol from one of the fifty states on the reverse side.

You also write checks on your bank account. A check is an order telling your bank to make a payment on your behalf. Your landlord cannot spend your check but must instead deposit it into, or "cash" it at, a bank. Your bank will make a payment to the landlord's bank – something that is called "check clearing" that we'll get to in a moment.

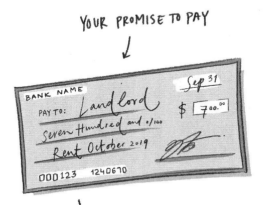

YOUR PROMISE TO PAY
↓

↓ ENDORSED BY A
BANK THAT WILL MAKE
THE PAYMENT FOR YOU.

If you are like me, you probably skip the checks and set up automatic payments at your bank, or use "plastic" (credit card).

After COVID, it is more common to make "touchless payments" through Smartphone readers that are equipped with a Near Field Communication (NFC) device to transfer payment information via what is called *Inductive Coupling*. I suppose that is the opposite of the *conscious uncoupling* that Gwyneth Paltrow and Chris Martin went through. If you find that sort of thing stimulating, go for it.

FLASH YOUR PHONE
AT AN ELECTRONIC READER
FOR SOME INDUCTIVE
COUPLING

So, what the heck is money? Paper? Metal? Plastic? Inductive coupling?

Modern research locates money's origins in the ancient temples of Babylonia, created for record-keeping – tracking the food provisions owed to workers in the temple.

MONEY'S ORIGINS "ARE LOST IN THE MISTS WHEN THE ICE WAS MELTING AND ...THE WEATHER WAS DELIGHTFUL AND THE MIND FREE TO BE FERTILE OF NEW IDEAS."

– JM KEYNES

Indeed, writing was probably invented by those early Babylonian accountants, with the records kept in *cuneiform* on clay *shubati* tablets. Let that sink in: accountants created writing, not poets.

Advanced math – too. Babylonian accountants knew how to calculate compound interest on debts. Without modern calculators!

While we imagine that the use of credit – say, installment credit to finance purchase of a new fridge – is a modern invention, actually from time immemorial most purchases were based on credit. Meaning, someone had to keep records of debts.

These debts had to be a) **denominated** in a measuring unit and b) **recorded** so that no one could forget.

You know what a measuring unit is – an inch, a cup, a pound (or, a centimeter, a liter, a kilogram for our European friends). But the kinds of debts we are talking about had to be measured in a *monetary* measuring unit – what we call a *money of account*. If we are going to find a way to measure both a goat and keg of beer, we cannot use length, volume, or weight. Today in America, of course, we use the *dollar* to measure in *money terms* the value of the goat and beer.

In ancient times, the money of account typically borrowed the name of the weight of a grain such as wheat or barley – hence the name for the money was derived from the name of the weight measure used for the most important grain.

Interestingly enough, the British still use the word *pound* to identify their money unit. Italy still used the word *lira* (which means pound in Italian) until switching to the euro. Ancient weight units mentioned in the Bible were the *mina*, the *talent*, and the *shekel* – all of which were adopted as the names of early money units.

Early debts were recorded in these monies of account – the *mina*, the *talent*, the *shekel*. The earliest debts, from Babylonia, were recorded on the clay tablets mentioned earlier.

Babylonian religious authorities also posted money values of goods and services on the temple's columns. These established prices for commonly traded items.

Maybe 5 *mina* for a goat and 6 *mina* for a keg of beer, for example. If I traded my goat for your keg of beer, I'd owe you 1 *mina* (6 − 5 = 1). We'd record this debt, denominated in *mina* (not goats or beer).

As another example, Babylonian "ale wives" kept track of beer debts on the "bar tab" (slate board behind the bar) in the money of account – say, one *mina* for every ten beers you drank.

BEER DEBTS RECORDED IN
"CHALK ON SLATE"

Beer debts were settled at the end of the growing season by turning over a portion of your barley harvest that she'd use to make the next batch of beer. If you owed

5 *mina* and a basket of barley was worth 2.5 *mina*, you would deliver two baskets of grain to settle your debt.

The technology used to keep these money records evolved over the next forty centuries, from clay, to ink on paper, stamped metal coins, and – finally! – electronic entries on computer hard-drives.

European monarchs preferred the technological innovation of notched tally sticks. We still use the term "score" (a wide notch to indicate the sum of 20) in sports (as a record of runs, for example, in baseball), and to indicate "scoring" wood.

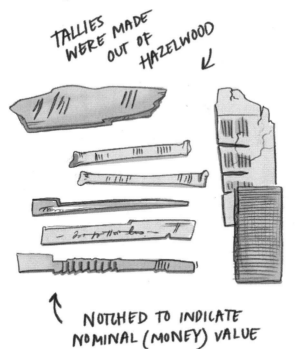

TALLIES MADE WERE OUT OF HAZELWOOD

NOTCHED TO INDICATE NOMINAL (MONEY) VALUE

These were an updated version of putting marks in clay. And, by splitting the sticks, both creditor and debtor would each retain a record.

You may remember Abe Lincoln's "four score and seven years ago" (eighty-seven years) in the Gettysburg Address. That term "score" comes from that ancient practice of notching a tally stick. And we still "tally up" our expenses as well as our points in card games.

Keep those tallies in mind.

3

Money: The Story of Redemption

Now we know where money came from. It originated in debts, denominated in a money of account.

Let's turn to the story of *redemption*: how you redeem yourself – that is, get yourself out of debt.

How about beginning with pizza? Everybody likes pizza! Believe it or not a pizza coupon is a lot like money. You can redeem one for a free pizza!

JOE'S PIZZA JOINT ISSUES FREE COUPONS

That coupon is a debt of Joe's Pizzeria – he owes you a pizza. You bring it into Joe's and exchange it for pizza.

You're happy – you got a free pizza. Joe's happy – he no longer owes a pizza and maybe he's gained a faithful customer who will return and spend dollars rather than coupons.

Now what will Joe do with the coupon? That coupon was his IOU ("I owe you a pizza"). Do you think he'll put it in the cash register and tally it up along with the George Washington notes he received from paying customers? Of course not. He's going to toss it into his wood-fired pizza oven.

YOU "REDEEM" THE COUPON FOR PIZZA

For you, that coupon represented a claim on a pizza – a type of "money" you can exchange for pizza.

For Joe, once *redeemed*, it is just trash.

This is a fundamental principle of accounting. When your IOU is returned to you in redemption, it is trash. Burn it.

What does redemption mean? Getting out of debt. Believe it or not, it does have a religious connotation. In the Semitic language spoken by Jesus, the word for both sin and debt is the same. You seek redemption for both sins and debts.

OK, but what does that have to do with money? Remember the tally sticks with "scores" (notches) that recorded money value?

You may have heard the phrase "raise a tally," which is what a king would do to purchase supplies for his army. This would be a call on the exchequer (the British Treasury) to notch and split sticks into a stock and a stub.

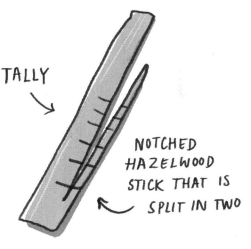

TALLY

NOTCHED HAZELWOOD STICK THAT IS SPLIT IN TWO

The exchequer could then "spend" the stub in payment to a supplier of the king. Say the king needed a mule that cost 20 pounds. A tally stick with one "score" (a notch indicating 20 pounds) would be split, with the exchequer keeping the stock and paying the seller of the mule with the stub. The seller would then either keep the stub or use it to pay his own debts.

At tax time, the exchequer would go to each village and collect the tally stubs in tax payments due, carefully matching them with the king's stocks (the other halves of the tallies).

Why match them? To ensure no one had counterfeited (that is, had added some extra "scores" – like adding zeros onto your dollar bill to increase the value to a hundred bucks).

Once the two halves of a tally matched, the tax was paid. And after all the tallies were collected, the exchequer would burn them to ensure no one could reuse them in payment.

Tally sticks were gradually phased out and replaced with metal coins. The British exchequer grew tired of the hassle of collecting, matching, and then burning the tallies. Finally, in 1834 the exchequer threw the last of the tally sticks into the fire in the Palace of Westminster (home to Parliament) with such gusto that the fire got out of control and burned much of the building!

KEEP THAT FIRE IN MIND. THEY BURNED THE TALLIES.

Let's look at a more recent example closer to home: the American colonies (before the revolution in 1776 that created the United States). The clever American colonists introduced to

23

the West a monetary innovation: paper currency. (The Chinese had used paper money for centuries before that – the West lagged behind.)

As colonies, they were expected to use British coins – and were forbidden to mint their own. Always short of British coins, the colonies passed laws authorizing the printing of paper notes – say, 10,000 Virginian *pounds'* worth – to be used for government spending. (Note: the name for their money of account was the pound – borrowed from Britain – but after the Revolution of 1776 Americans replaced it with the *dollar*.)

AMERICAN
COLONIAL PAPER
MONEY

FIFTY SHILLINGS

No.0332
FIFTY SHILLINGS
According to an Act of General
Assembly of Pennsylvania,
passed in the
13th Year of the
Reign of his
Majesty Geo the
Third. Dated
the first of
October, 1773.

Beny morgan

B Barnes.

Fifty Shillings

20 SHILLINGS
= 1 POUND

At the same time, they would pass a tax law expected to raise 10,000 *pounds* of tax revenue.

These obligations were called "redemption taxes."

Once spent into the economy, taxpayers could use the notes to pay the taxes. The colonial governments kept careful records of spending and taxing, and these show that about three-fourths of the notes would return as tax revenue.

When the notes were received as tax revenue, the colonial government burned them.

Let's repeat that. The colonial governments burned all their tax revenue.

Do you see a pattern? Revenue. Redemption. Fire.

Interestingly, our word *revenue* was derived from French and means "return to." What returned? The paper notes that had been spent by the government.

ALL THE RETURNED NOTES WERE BURNED.

Like tally sticks and pizza coupons, once returned to their issuer, the paper money tax revenue was burned. That is what they meant by "redemption taxes."

The tally stick or paper money was "redeemed" and burned when taxes were paid.

Redemption! When redeemed, the taxpayer no longer owed taxes. At the same time, the colonial government was no longer obligated to accept its currency in payment – because the money was redeemed and burned.

Both taxer and taxpayer were redeemed. Simultaneously. Hallelujah!

This concept of redemption seems strange at first, so let's look at one final example.

You can take a tour of one of the Federal Reserve's district banks (there are twelve of them, spread around in cities across the USA, including Boston, San Francisco, and Chicago), and at the end of the tour you will get a little baggie filled with shredded green paper money. It might have included "Benjamins" ($100 bills)!

You mean the Fed just shreds its money? Isn't that an insane waste of "taxpayer money"? Why didn't they spend it instead?

SHREDDING BENJAMINS
AT THE FED.

Those paper notes are the liabilities of the Fed – that is why they are called Federal Reserve notes. Sort of like Joe's coupons.

If *you* hold some pizza coupons or $100 Benjamins, they are assets – something you can save or spend. When Fed notes are received at the Fed, they are just pieces of paper – like Joe's coupons that have been "redeemed."

While it is true that the Fed could keep some on a shelf to be reissued (and, to tell the truth, Joe could do the same with his pizza coupons), when they are at the Fed, they are not counted as assets. They are just pieces of paper.

They are valuable only when they are *not* at the Fed – that is, when they are in *your* hands. Because when they are in your hands, they are the Fed's IOU and your asset.

The same is true of Joe's coupons – they have no value when Joe has them, but they are worth a pizza in *your* hands. It would be silly and a bit schizoid for Joe to use his own coupons, to demand from himself a pizza! They are his IOUs.

Same for the Fed: its notes are its IOUs. When returned to the Fed, they can be shredded.

Joe can always print up more pizza coupons to issue to potential customers. The Fed can always print up more paper notes to issue. Strangely enough, neither Joe nor the Fed can run out.

But don't try this at home! If you try to print and spend fake Federal Reserve notes, you go to prison.

4

Currency:
The Government's Money

So far we've seen that:

1 Money takes many forms (tallies, coins, notes, checks), but it's really just an IOU – like a pizza coupon.
2 As with any IOU, it can be shredded or burned once it is returned to its issuer.

But what does that mean for the dollar bill? Is that just an IOU as well? Who owes whom what?

Imagine you are king of your own kingdom. (Nice!) But you fear your neighboring king might invade. (Not so nice!) You need to build walls around your castle. You need mules and workers to bring bricks and skilled bricklayers to build the walls.

Just your luck, there's a village close by with workers and mules, and you happen to be the sovereign king, with sovereign power that mere mortals do not usually possess. A king can impose fees, fines, taxes, tithes, and tribute on his subjects. As king, you can decide what you'll accept in payment. And you've got the sword to enforce payments.

PENALTY FOR NON-PAYMENT CAN BE SEVERE

You decide that you'll mint some new coins – with *your* face on the front, of course. You announce they are each worth one *ducat* (the name of a medieval Italian coin – sounds more sophisticated than just calling them "Johnsons," after your last name).

You plan to hire workers and buy donkeys with the coins. But why would anyone take them?

Because you put a tax on all the villagers – each owes 1 *ducat* in tax for each month until the wall is completed.

They've got to get coins to pay their taxes – and you are the only issuer of the coins, so they must get them from you. Voila!

It isn't really money that governments need – remember, they burn (or melt) the revenue, anyway. They need the mules, wagons, soldiers, and sailors. They use their currency to buy what they really need. But governments must find a way to induce subjects or citizens to exchange their stuff (say, mules) for government's currency.

We already mentioned the redemption taxes imposed by American colonial governments, payable in the paper notes they issued. And the wooden tally sticks issued by European monarchs.

Metal coins were invented about seven centuries before Christ and used alongside tallies in medieval Europe.

In each case, sovereign governments imposed taxes and other obligations, issued their own IOUs as currency, then accepted the currency in payment of taxes, fees, and fines.

Sometimes they also enforced use among others in private transactions. They would mandate their coins to be used as "legal tender" – a practice that has carried

KINGS ISSUED COINS, SPENT THEM, AND ACCEPTED THEM AS PAYMENT

through to the Fed's own notes, as we saw earlier. Pronouncing that the coins were "legal tender" meant that they must be accepted for all payments – both to pay debts and also to buy stuff.

Penalties for non-acceptance could be severe, up to and including death. Presumably severe punishment was a pretty good incentive to accept the coins – but you had to be caught refusing them. If caught, you might have a red-hot coin burned into your forehead to serve as a warning to others!

Still, if nearly everyone has to make payments to the crown, the crown's coins will be widely accepted – since everyone can pay liabilities such as fees, fines, and taxes with those coins.

And since the king would outlaw just about everything commoners needed to do for survival (such as hunting deer and cutting firewood in Sherwood Forest of Robin Hood lore), just about everyone needed coins to keep out of the dungeon.

However, we should not deny the benefits of the use of coins. They could also be used in commerce – which grew significantly as coins became plentiful.

So, to recap: the sovereign king issues a currency (stamped coins, scored tallies, printed paper notes), uses it to purchase goods and services, imposes tax obligations, and redeems the currency in tax payments. And then burns or melts down the revenue.

COINAGE, TAXATION, REDEMPTION

As shorthand, we can put it this way: "taxes drive money," in the sense that the need to pay obligations to the sovereign authority (today mostly taxes, although fees, fines, tribute, or tithes can also work) induces the subjects (in a monarchy) or citizens (in a democracy) to offer goods and services for sale in order to get the money needed to pay the obligations.

The taxpayers "redeem" themselves, getting out of debt, while the authority "redeems" the currency by accepting it in payment.

Today in America, we've got a democracy – no monarch, but our elected representatives impose taxes in dollars. On tax day we pay the IRS. We'll see later what forms of money we use today to redeem ourselves as we pay taxes.

THE NEED TO PAY TAXES MEANS...
THAT PEOPLE WORK TO GET THAT
IN WHICH TAXES ARE PAID.

Those who owe taxes will work or sell stuff to obtain the government's money – which they can use to pay taxes.

Look at it this way. Government needs resources. In the bad old days of monarchies, the resources were largely squandered supporting the crown's lifestyle.

Today, democracies expect government to serve the public purpose – that is, to spend to help *us*.

To do so, governments largely rely on resources provided by the nongovernment sectors – households and business firms. That is, by *us* – businesses that supply goods and services and workers that produce them.

Consider the alternative. Back in the old days of monarchies, you'd go out to the pub for a beer. You might drink a wee bit too much.

Government needs some sailors for the navy. You wake up the next morning to find you'd been conscripted into the navy.

"YOU'RE IN THE NAVY NOW!"

So, taxes might be the least worst way to move resources to the government.

Rather than simply seizing whatever it needs – mules, wagons, and soldiers – government can use money to pay for them. You can voluntarily sell to the government if you think the price is right.

However, you are going to have to pay those taxes – or face a penalty.

5

Can Government Run Out of Currency?

Let's recap what we've learned so far.

1 Money is really just an IOU denominated in a money of account.
2 Government can impose obligations – such as taxes – payable in its own IOUs, called currency.
3 It can spend its currency to hire workers and pay for supplies it needs.
4 Like any other issuer of an IOU, government can shred its currency when received in tax payments.

This raises another question: if dollars are just our government's IOUs, does that mean Uncle Sam cannot run out of dollars?

That's right!

Remember, Pizza Joe cannot run out of his coupons. He

might run out of pizza, but not out of coupons.

Many people do not realize this – even many economists and politicians do not. But some are coming around to the idea – as we will see.

In this chapter we'll look at some famous – and not so famous – economists and even a former president to see what they've said about government's money.

"CURRENCY:
THAT WHICH IS
NEEDED TO
PAY TAXES"

In 1996 a hedge fund guy named Warren Mosler introduced this big idea to a group of economists: government doesn't need tax revenue in order to spend. Rather, *we need the government's currency* so that we can pay taxes.

Warren is an expert in government bonds – he specialized in trading them – so he understood a lot about government finances. And he realized that most people get those finances the wrong way around.

Government is the source of the currency. Government must spend currency before we – the taxpayers – can use it to pay taxes. So, government doesn't spend tax revenue. What are taxes really for? To create a demand for the currency!

With the recognition that taxes drive the demand for currency, and with the further realization that government must spend its currency before collecting taxes, came the shocking conclusion that government doesn't need tax revenue to finance its spending!

Well, duh! Government burns its revenue. There's nothing left to spend!

But Warren wasn't the first to recognize this obvious point.

Indeed, right after World War II, the governor of the New York Fed went around the country preaching that "taxes for revenue purposes are obsolete!"

His name was Beardsley Ruml. (You cannot make that up. And, no, he didn't have a beard.)

What he meant was that, while taxes might be important for other purposes, we don't need no stinking taxes to finance government spending. Indeed, government doesn't spend tax revenue, government burns it.

"TAXATION FOR REVENUE IS OBSOLETE."

— RUML, 1946

BEARDSLEY RUML

But if that is true, how does the government finance its spending?

Interestingly enough, two other well-known Fed heads recently provided hints in separate Congressional testimonies.

Fed Chairman Alan Greenspan was known for his super-duper free market orientation. Even before he was at the Fed, he was chosen by President Ronald Reagan in the mid-1980s to "reform" the Social Security program,* which many feared would soon run out of money.

You see, a flood of retirements would soon begin as the baby boomers (born during the two decades following World War II) reached age sixty-five. So, as head of that commission, Greenspan advocated big payroll tax increases to raise revenue that would be set aside to be used later for baby boomer retirements.

(Well, later arrived! We are half-way through the boomer retirements right now.)

"THERE'S NOTHING THAT PREVENTS THE FEDERAL GOVERNMENT FROM PRINTING AS MUCH MONEY AS IT WANTS TO PRINT."

*Created in the 1930s, Social Security provides monthly income for retired workers. It also taxes workers and their employers – through a payroll tax. The tax supposedly "pays for" the retirements. But, as Greenspan later admitted, taxes are not necessary to pay the benefits.

Even though taxes were raised, handwringing about Social Security's ability to pay benefits resurfaced in the 1990s. By then, Greenspan chaired the Fed. He was brought before Congress and asked point-blank by Congressman Paul Ryan about the potential bankruptcy of Social Security.

Amazingly, this time he said "nope." Government can make all payments as they come due by "printing as much money as it wants to print."

But can lightning strike twice? Yes, indeed it can. Skip forward a few years. Ben Bernanke replaced Greenspan at the helm of the Fed. He was hauled in before Congress after the Fed's rescue of financial institutions in the aftermath of the Global Financial Crisis. The Fed had lent and spent a total of $29 trillion to save the financial system.

BERNANKE

That is trillion with a capital T. Twenty-nine followed by twelve zeros. Congress was furious. Congress wanted to know where Bernanke got all that money. Was it taxpayer's money?

PELLEY: "IS THAT TAX MONEY THAT THE FED IS SPENDING?"

BERNANKE: "ITS NOT TAX MONEY. WE SIMPLY USE THE COMPUTER TO MARK UP THE SIZE OF THE ACCOUNT."

Nope. Bernanke calmly explained that the Fed has this new invention – a computer – and all he had to do was to keystroke $29 trillion into existence. The Fed simply created the money. No taxes required.

Government doesn't spend tax revenue.

And, yet, when President Obama was asked why the government couldn't do more to help "Main Street" recover from the global financial crisis, he responded that he'd love to do that but the government had run out of money!

Few politicians seemed to have paid attention to what Ruml, Mosler, Greenspan, and Bernanke had said. Government cannot run out of money!

And, yet, lightning struck again in 2020 when the COVID pandemic hit our economy. First President Trump and then President Biden got Congress to authorize pandemic relief, to a total of $5 trillion! Thousands of dollars' worth of checks were sent out to anyone who could fog a mirror.

Where did Congress find the money? Keystroked by the Fed's computers.

Those funds helped to support Americans in their time of need – they could keep the electricity on, pay their rents and mortgages, and put food on the table. The pandemic recession was deep, but recovery began quickly.

However, it soon became apparent that Congress doesn't really understand, because, after passing the pandemic relief package, politicians backtracked and refused to pass President Biden's proposal to update America's infrastructure – electricity grid, highways and railroads, schools, airports, and bridges.

Many said it costs too much. Government doesn't have the money and we cannot ask taxpayers to pay for it.

Unfortunately, the COVID pandemic did not end quickly. America still needed more government help to fund healthcare, research into vaccine improvement, and purchasing of safety and testing equipment. And more relief for those who couldn't work but were facing eviction from their homes.

No more help came because Congress couldn't find the money!

When politicians understand that Uncle Sam can always find money, they can improve the lives of citizens. When they don't, it's like tying Uncle Sam's arms behind his back and sending him into the boxing ring.

Let us now reflect on remarks made by someone who does understand government finance, Congressman John Yarmuth, chair of the House Budget Committee.

"WE ISSUE OUR OWN CURRENCY, AND WE CAN SPEND ENOUGH TO MEET THE NEEDS OF THE AMERICAN PEOPLE."

That might sound like a boring, sleep-inducing assignment to head a bunch of humorless number-crunching bureaucrats. But that is where all the action is.

The Budget Committee is responsible for ushering all spending and tax bills through Congress – and, if approved, then the committee works with the Senate and the president to make them law. All that pandemic relief flowed through Yarmuth's hands – all $5 trillion.

And Yarmuth understands money, as he showed in an amazing interview on C-Span in 2021:

> **Historically, what we've always done is said, "What can we *afford* to do?" And that's not the right question. The right question is, "*What do the American People need us to do?*" And *that* question becomes the first question. Once you answered *that*, then you say, "*How do you resource that need?*"**

We issue our own currency, and we can spend enough to meet the needs of the American people – the only constraint is finding the resources needed to satisfy the needs.

He got it right.

Today, as we face climate catastrophe, a continuing global health pandemic, refugee crises, rising sea levels, forever fires, poverty, and homelessness, we need to teach our politicians that Uncle Sam can indeed find the money he needs to mount a response.

We've got the money. We've got the resources. All we need to do is to quicken the will of our elected representatives so that they will do the right thing.

6

Anyone Can Create Money?

The previous chapters have highlighted the government's own money – what we call sovereign currency. However, we have also discussed bank checks and even pizza coupons. And we talked about "bar tabs" that record the debts of pub patrons.

Money is always a debt – but a specific kind of debt: a debt denominated in money. That is, a promise to pay money. Not a promise to pay pizza! And anyone can write I,O,U!

HYMAN P. MINSKY
1919 - 1996

If you don't believe it yet, take it from my professor, Hyman Minsky, who used to always say: "Anyone can create money."

Wow. Anyone? Yes, anyone. Including you!

All you have to do is write "I Owe You Five Bucks."

"ANYONE CAN CREATE MONEY..."

But, before you get too excited, Minsky warned that the problem is to get your money accepted.

What was Minsky getting at? Money is always and everywhere a debt of its issuer – an IOU. And it is a credit of the holder – a You-Owe-Me from the creditor's view.

Two sides of the same coin, so to speak.

But *you* cannot make someone hold your IOU – they must be willing creditors.

There are two important aspects of debts. First, when you write an IOU you specify its *denomination*. You might write:

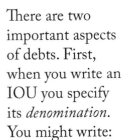

" THE PROBLEM IS GETTING IT ACCEPTED."

"IOU a cup of sugar." Your debt is denominated in sugar. You are promising to pay sugar. That's not a money debt.

Second, you record the debt by writing it on a slip of paper (think of the pizza coupon – the pizza joint wrote its pizza debt on paper). Your neighbor holds your IOU as a record of the debt.

We've already talked about records on clay tablets, notched tally sticks, stamped coins, and computer hard-drives. That's all about technology, which changes over time.

MONEY IS A RECORD OF DEBT

What doesn't change is that money is always a recorded debt.

When you repay your sugar debt, your neighbor returns to you the record of your sugar IOU.

What do you do with it? You tear it up, of course! That's the act of redemption. You are no longer in debt.

The same is true when you write an IOU in terms of money: IOU $5. When you do pay down your debt by delivering five bucks, your IOU is returned and you destroy it.

So, you can write "sugar debts" and you can also write "money debts." They are IOUs denominated in sugar or money, respectively.

But acceptability is key. You can probably get family members and close friends to accept your IOU. But without close personal relations, finding acceptance is difficult.

The stranger has doubts you'll pay up.

IOUs require special characteristics to increase acceptability. Let's briefly examine three: transferability; liquidity; yield. These can make your monetary IOU more acceptable.

TRANSFERABILITY,
LIQUIDITY, AND YIELD
INCREASE ACCEPTABILITY

Transferability means that a monetary IOU can pass from hand to hand. Let's say you write an IOU $5 to your mom. She accepts it because she believes you are good for the debt. She owes your brother five bucks for doing some yard work. She pays him with your IOU. He accepts it because . . . well, because he's your brother. Now you owe him.

Essentially, your mom used your IOU as money to pay her own debt. You pay your brother the five bucks, you receive back your IOU, and you tear it up.

The key point here is that, if your IOU is acceptable, your creditor can use your IOU to make a purchase from someone else or to pay down a monetary debt owed to someone other than you – in either case transferring your IOU to someone else.

Getting someone to endorse your IOU increases acceptability. The endorser promises to make the payment if you fail to do so. It helps if that endorser is well known, well heeled, and highly respected. Maybe your buddy is Elon Musk? He endorses your IOU and then people outside your family will take it. If you default on your promise, Elon is on the hook.

Out in the real world, banks, central banks, and government treasuries are the most common endorsers. If Uncle Sam stands behind your IOU, you are good to go. Believe it or not, Uncle Sam does stand behind many people's promises to pay their home mortgage debts – and that makes their mortgages quite acceptable to creditors!

Liquidity means that an IOU can be exchanged quickly for currency (the IOU of the government) with little loss of value. The deposits in your checking account are highly liquid – you just need to go to the ATM machine to convert them to cash.

A ninety-day certificate of deposit is less liquid – there's a substantial penalty for early withdrawal (meaning, a loss of value).

What about *yield*? A lot of monetary IOUs promise to pay interest – that's called *yield* (earnings from holding an IOU). Maybe your creditor will demand that you pay 10 percent interest on your IOU – your $5 IOU requires a payment of $5.50 to get yourself out of debt.

So . . . it is not quite so simple as it first seemed. Yes, anyone can write "IOU five bucks," but getting it accepted might require endorsement, access to the ATM, and paying interest.

For many purposes, it makes sense to argue that, while many IOUs can be denominated in money (i.e.: written in money terms), it is best to reserve the term "money" for those IOUs that are both denominated in money and highly *acceptable* – because they are transferable and liquid.

Such IOUs generally pay little to no interest precisely because they are highly liquid; IOUs that are not so liquid (such as a ninety-day CD) must pay higher interest. Paying the higher interest rate can make a less liquid asset more acceptable.

If we narrowly restrict the term in that manner, we'd probably say that, while anyone can write an IOU in money terms, most individuals cannot *create money*.

ANYONE CAN CREATE
A MONETARY IOU, BUT ONLY
SOME QUALIFY AS MONEY

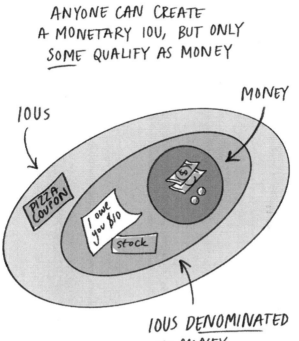

In that case, we'd reserve the term "money" for only a subset of all the money-denominated debts. Maybe we would limit it to money IOUs issued by government and banks, and – just maybe – by other kinds of financial institutions – such as money market mutual funds.

7

Private Bank Money

What we've learned so far:

1 Money takes many forms, but it's always an IOU.
2 US dollars are money-denominated IOUs written by Uncle Sam; he can shred them when returned in tax payments.
3 You could also create your own money if you can get it accepted.

But the bad news is that the only way you could create your own money and have it widely accepted is if you got someone really trustworthy (like Uncle Sam) to endorse your money and back it up.

Uncle Sam has no problem getting his IOUs accepted, of course. And we need his IOUs because we've got to pay taxes to him.

WE ALL ACCEPT
UNCLE SAM'S IOUS!

And he stands firmly behind chartered banks – they've got Federal Deposit Insurance Corporation liabilities that are guaranteed by the "full faith and credit" of the government. You've seen the FDIC logo on the doors of your bank telling you that Uncle Sam stands behind your deposits.

The FDIC's promise makes your deposits at the bank perfectly safe. If your bank cannot, or refuses to, let you withdraw cash from your deposit account, the FDIC will pay you. It wasn't always so – as we'll explain later in chapter 8.

BACKED BY THE US GOVERNMENT,
EACH DEPOSITOR IS INSURED
AT LEAST $250,000

That makes insured bank deposits highly acceptable. You can write checks that will be accepted almost everywhere.

Bank deposits are liabilities of the bank, IOUs to you, their creditor. Bank Owes You! What does the bank owe you? The right to "demand" cash in exchange for a deduction to your "demand deposit" (the technical name for a checking deposit).

You probably never knew that you are the bank's creditor, and they are your debtor!

To be clear, when you write a check, you are not creating money – you are using bank money. The recipient will deposit your check in their own bank and receive a credit to their demand deposit.

Their bank will present evidence of your check either to your bank for clearing or (more likely) send it on to the Central Bank (the Federal Reserve Bank – or Fed – in the USA) for clearing. (Explained in the next chapter.)

How and why do banks create their money IOUs? Mostly to make loans.

Let's say your dream has been to open a bakery. You've inherited a small building downtown, fixed it up nicely, put up a sign and are ready to get down to business. You need some basic equipment and supplies like flour and yeast.

ALL YOU NEED NOW IS A COMMERCIAL LOAN

You go to your local bank that specializes in commercial (small business) loans. You bring all your documents to satisfy the loan officer that you deserve a loan of $25,000 to get into business. The loan officer examines your *prospectus* as part of the underwriting process.

You convince the lender that you are a good credit risk with little chance of default. You sign the loan contract (or "note") agreeing to repay the loan on schedule, with interest. A demand deposit account is opened in your name and you are allowed to spend up to the agreed limit. (This will be something like a revolving line of credit – you'll be able to write checks as you spend to furnish the bakery, up to the total $25,000 limit.)

Where did the bank get the money to lend? It created it – as an IOU – and credited your deposit account.

YOU BRING A BUSINESS PLAN. THEY
CHECK IF THEY ARE WORTHY OF CREDIT.

Remember, your bank deposit is the bank's IOU and you are the creditor.

But, wait a minute – how did you, a borrower, turn the tables and somehow become the bank's *creditor*?

Well, you *still* are a borrower, and you owe the bank $25 grand plus interest. But you are also a creditor: the bank has promised to cover your spending up to $25,000, crediting its IOUs to your deposit account so that you can write checks.

The bank is also both a debtor (your demand deposit) and a creditor (your loan "note"). It balances – you are both simultaneously debtors and creditors.

SOME LOANS WILL GO INTO DEFAULT;
LOSSES ARE COVERED BY THE
BANK'S INTEREST EARNINGS

Well, it almost balances. You can borrow and spend up
to $25,000, but you will end up repaying the bank more
than $25,000 because you pay interest. The bank uses
that to cover business costs plus gross profits and losses.

This seems almost magical! Where does money come
from? Can banks just create it out of thin air?

Yes, they can. But remember that anyone can create
money – the problem is to get it accepted.

Banks are backstopped by Uncle Sam. Their word
is good. Mostly. If the bank should fail, Uncle Sam
will make their IOU deposits good – paying off the
depositors with Uncle Sam's checks.

To complete the story of bank money creation, suppose you've saved a down payment for a new house. You go see the loan officer. You bring all the necessary documents showing your income and credit history.

Hurray! Your mortgage loan is approved: $350,000

YOU NEED A MORTGAGE TO BUY A HOUSE

from the bank, $50,000 from your down payment, and you get the house for $400k. You've got a thirty-year mortgage at a fixed interest rate of 4 percent. You sign a mortgage "note," promising to pay monthly.

LOOKING FORWARD TO REDEMPTION DAY!

For the next thirty years you faithfully make payments, looking forward to that final payment when the house is all yours, free and clear. You have three kids, watch them grow up and move away; you switch jobs several times; and you grow older, approaching retirement.

The fateful day finally arrives. You make that last payment. The bank returns your note. You call all your friends and family over!

Yep, you burn the note. IOUs are always toasted when returned to the issuer.

8

The Central Bank's Money: Lender of Last Resort

We've mentioned that central banks clear checks between banks. In this chapter we will look at that in more detail and also consider another responsibility of central banks: acting as lender of last resort. That has to do with supporting private banks – making them safe.

THE FED CLEARS CHECKS
BETWEEN BANKS

Central banks have long issued paper notes – much like our Federal Reserve notes today. In addition to financing the spending of governments, those notes also were used by private banks for "clearing."

Let's explain how private banks used central bank notes for clearing back in the old days. Until a century ago, many private banks also issued notes – private paper money. They would issue notes when they made loans. The notes were their IOUs and could be used by borrowers to make purchases or to pay down debt. The private bank notes circulated alongside central bank notes and also treasury notes and coins.

The private banks accumulated central bank notes by accepting them in payment of loans. They could also make their own bank notes more acceptable by promising to redeem their notes for the central bank's notes. This is what led to use of central bank notes for "clearing" between banks.

Let's look at the example of private banking in eighteenth-century England and the relation of private banks with the Bank of England, which became England's central bank. Like other banks of that time, the Bank of England issued paper notes in its lending business (some of those loans were to the king or queen, while other loans went to businesses and banks).

If you owed, say, the Bank of Nottingham a payment on a loan, you could make that payment using a Bank of

BANK OF ENGLAND ;
100 POUNDS

England note. You are no longer in debt, and the Bank of Nottingham can hold the Bank of England note as its asset.

Or, if you were the Bank of Nottingham and received a note issued by the Bank of Liverpool, you could ask that bank to pay you using Bank of England notes. When the Bank of Liverpool pays using a Bank of England note, the Bank of Liverpool will receive back its own note in redemption – at which point, the note is burned.

In other words, Bank of England notes could be used for "clearing accounts" among banks.

The problem was that a bank could run out of Bank of England notes to be used for such clearing. As word spread that, say, the Bank of Nottingham was short of

66

them, there could be a "run" on its own notes (holders of them would try to exchange them for Bank of England notes). Once Nottingham ran out of Bank of England notes, it would have to shut its doors because it could no longer make the promised conversion.

This run could spread to notes of other banks – after all, if one bank could run out of Bank of England notes and be forced to default, another bank might do so, too. The promises to redeem one's bank notes for Bank of England notes would be broken – that is a default and breaks the trust in banks.

RUNS SPREAD QUICKLY!
NO BANK CAN SURVIVE
ONE WITHOUT HELP.

To stop a run, the Bank of England could lend its own notes to banks needing them. Since the Bank of England could always print more, it would not run out. This activity is called "lender of last resort" and became the classic policy to stop bank runs.

In a lender of last resort operation, the central bank lends its own notes so private banks can redeem *their* notes for the central bank's notes. This stops the run. Gradually, the central bank notes will flow back into private banks as loans are repaid and banks then can repay their loans to the central bank.

Lender of last resort operations became the second function of central banking – the first was to finance government (a topic of the next chapter), and the second was to serve as lender of last resort to back-up private banks.

Over time, banks switched from issuing notes as their main IOU to issuing deposits (as they do today). They would promise to convert deposits to central bank notes *on demand* (hence, the term "demand deposits"). They also would use central bank liabilities – central bank notes and reserves – to clear checks with other banks.

What are reserves? They are simply deposit accounts that private banks have at their central bank. The central bank just keystrokes those reserves into the accounts of the banks that need them, as a loan to be repaid later. Today, banks clear checks with one another using reserves, not central bank notes.

Most of the more developed nations had central banks to operate as lenders of last resort by the end of the nineteenth century, but not the USA! As a consequence, bank runs and severe financial crises were common – there was no lender of last resort.

This happened about once a generation in the USA throughout the nineteenth century. After a banking panic in 1907, the biggest banks got together and demanded that Congress create a central bank – the Federal Reserve Bank – through legislation in 1913.

The Fed was specifically created to ensure "par clearing": so a $100 check drawn against one bank would be accepted at other banks at the value of $100. And you would always be able to withdraw cash (Federal Reserve notes) against your deposit.

CITI'S $100 CHECK
CLEARS AT A PAR OF $100
AGAINST CHASE'S

This *should* have stopped bank runs. But it *didn't*.

Bank runs returned with a vengeance during the 1930s Great Depression, as famously memorialized in the Jimmy Stewart film *It's a Wonderful Life*. In the movie, a competitor bank creates a run on the Bailey Brothers Building & Loan bank owned by Stewart.

He pleads with depositors to leave their deposits in his bank, stating the "money's not here. It's in Joe's house" – that is, the deposits are backed by the mortgages he's made in town, not by cash in the vault.

The experience of the Depression prodded the Fed to take more responsibility as a lender of last resort. In addition, Congress and President Roosevelt created the FDIC to insure deposits. Bank runs ended. We still get financial crises, and banks do occasionally fail, but depositors no longer have to worry about their savings.

Remember that we discussed the claim that "anyone can create money, but the problem is to get it accepted." Acceptability can be increased by getting your IOUs endorsed by someone who is trusted. We also talked about how the FDIC stands behind deposits of banks: if your bank fails, Uncle Sam uses the FDIC to pay you the full value of your deposits (up to a limit – now $250,000).

That makes you willing to accept "bank money" (bank checks and deposits).

However, the failure of a bank is a bit messy – it will take a while for the FDIC to get around to paying you. Besides, you are not just worried about being paid – eventually. Often, you want your money *right now*! And you want it in cash – good old George Washingtons ($1), Hamiltons ($10), and Benjamins ($100).

Those are all IOUs of the Fed. Your bank cannot issue them. Yes, banks store a few in the safe, and they fill the ATMs with them. But their stored cash is a tiny fraction of the deposit IOUs they've issued. If more than a few of their depositors all happened to show up at the same time, they'd run out very quickly. That's what happened to Jimmy Stewart.

BANKS HOLD VERY LITTLE
CASH AGAINST DEPOSITS

So central bankers and private bankers came up with a game plan. If they promise you that you can *always* get cash out, you'll see no need to take all the cash out. You trust that the Fed will always provide the cash your bank has promised to provide, so you never need to test whether that is true. And, if you never test, the bank never fails to provide it on demand!

This allows the banks to keep a small amount of cash on hand, always replenished by the Fed that sends armored trucks to restock the ATMs. They send extra trucks around Christmas when the demand for cash for shopping is always high.

With the Fed as lender of last resort, and with the FDIC guaranteeing the value of your deposits, you sleep soundly at night. Even though you (now) know your bank is holding hardly any cash.

When Willie Sutton – a famous and persistent bank robber – was asked why he robbed banks, he purportedly answered: "Because that's where the money is."

Well, not so much.

9

Central Bank Money: Government Finance

Central banks were originally created to finance government spending. In the distant past, governments spent directly: their treasuries would simply notch hazelwood sticks, stamp coins, or print paper money. With the rise of private banking and then central banks, things became a bit more complex. Now central banks are heavily involved in governments' spending – and so are private banks. Let's peel back the curtain to see how it works today.

As we know, governments originally spent their money first and then collected it from taxes. Spend first, then tax. It was obvious that government did not spend tax revenue, because they burned it!

The question many ask is this: do governments need tax money before they spend? No, governments must spend their currency before they can collect it in taxes.

WHICH CAME FIRST, SPENDING OR TAXES?

SPENDING!

But with the rise of banking and the creation of central banks, there are two degrees of separation between the population and the government: a central bank and private banks stand in the middle. It becomes more difficult to follow the process.

So, we must understand that most sovereign governments no longer spend their currency directly. Instead, just as you use a bank to make and receive payments, the government uses its bank – the central bank – to make and receive payments on its behalf.

We've already discussed the use of private banks: if you work for wages, you either get a paycheck or a direct payroll deposit; in either case, your demand deposit at your bank is credited. When you pay bills (either by check or electronic payment), your deposit is debited.

When the US Treasury spends (either by cutting a check or by electronic payment), it orders *the Fed* to make a payment on its behalf. The Fed will credit the reserves of the *bank* used by the recipient of Treasury spending.

Reserves are like a "checking account" that banks hold at the central bank.

So, as the Treasury spends, the Fed "keystrokes" a credit to the private bank's reserve account. The private bank then "keystrokes" a credit to the demand deposit of the recipient.

Today, all government spending takes that form: if you receive a government check and deposit it in your bank, your deposit account receives a credit, and your bank's reserves at the Fed are credited.

Note the two degrees of separation: the Fed and your private bank stand between you and the Treasury.

When a taxpayer (say, a household) pays taxes (writing a check or making an electronic payment), the household's bank will debit the taxpayer's deposit account and the central bank will debit the reserves of the bank the household uses.

So, the modern process of government spending and taxing uses central bank reserves (deposits at the central bank) rather than paper notes and coins; those reserves are effectively modern "currency" used by governments.

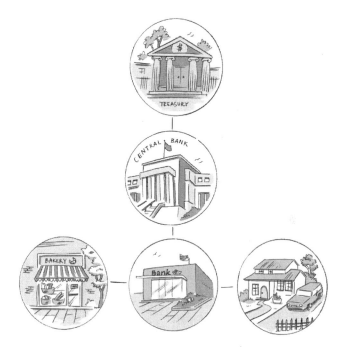

THE CENTRAL BANK RECEIVES
AND MAKES PAYMENTS ON
BEHALF OF THE TREASURY.

Governments don't need to push around wheelbarrows full of cash to make payments.

Spending puts reserves into the banking system; taxing takes them out. When government spending is greater than tax receipts, reserves in the banking system go up. Those represent a government IOU, but an asset of the private banks. In the next chapter we'll talk about that a bit more.

This raises the question: Where does the Fed get reserves from? It simply keystrokes them. It cannot run out.

It cannot run out of its Federal Reserve notes either: if banks need more for their ATM machines, the Fed prints them up, ships them in armored cars to the banks, and debits bank reserves. Reserves and paper currency are central bank IOUs, and the central bank can never run out. (*See the boxes at the end of this chapter.*)

Wait a minute. That means Uncle Sam can never run out of money?

PULL THOSE RESERVE RABBITS... ... OUT OF THE HAT!

Indeed, it does, as we said before. Once Congress and the president approve a budget, the Treasury can order the Fed to pull reserve rabbits out of its magician's hat to finance the spending authorized.

Recall that we earlier quoted two former chairmen of the Fed – Greenspan and Bernanke – who argued that Uncle Sam can never run out of keystrokes.

The Federal Reserve Bank of St Louis also weighed in: the US government can always pay its bills.

"AS THE SOLE MANUFACTURER OF DOLLARS WHOSE DEBT IS DENOMINATED IN DOLLARS, THE US GOVERNMENT CAN NEVER BECOME INSOLVENT."

Yet, we hear all the time that the government either *has* run out of money or will *soon* do so. It is common to make the claim that the government is just like a household. And, just like a household, if it continually spends more than its income, it will go bankrupt.

That cannot be true.

When government spends more than it receives in tax revenue, we call that a deficit. Government is issuing more of its IOUs than it "burns" as it receives tax payments.

The St Louis Fed says deficits cannot lead to insolvency. The Fed is right. But most people remain confused because they believe the "government is just like a household" false analogy.

THE BELIEF THAT GOVERNMENT,
LIKE A HOUSEHOLD, MUST BALANCE
ITS BUDGET IS A DANGEROUS MYTH.

Let's drop the myth and pursue truth. You can run out of money. A business firm can run out of money. A city – even New York City! – can run out of money. But Uncle Sam can't.

We'll dig deeper into government deficits and debt in the next chapter.

> *How does "cash" (paper notes and coins) get into the economy today? Mostly ATMs or bank tellers. Remember that demand deposits are redeemable "on demand" for cash – the bank promises to convert on demand. And the central bank promises that banks can always convert their reserves to cash "on demand." So, when a bank gets low on cash, it simply orders delivery via armored truck, and the central bank debits the bank's reserves.*

> *Here's a little-known fact. Coins are technically issued by the Treasury and represent its debt. You can pay your taxes due by pushing a wheelbarrow load of pennies to the Treasury's Internal Revenue Service (IRS) to make the payment. That would cut out the "middlemen" – the Fed and your private bank. But it would be a hassle for both you and the Treasury. However, the Treasury never spends by delivering pennies. It used to issue its own paper money – Treasury notes – so could cut the Fed out of the picture by printing up paper currency. But it stopped doing that decades ago. Today it only spends through that "middleman," the Fed.*

10

Government's Debt is Our Asset

In the previous chapter we learned that, if government spends more in a year than taxes received, that is called a deficit. We also saw that the Fed says deficits cannot lead to bankruptcy. Uncle Sam can always make all payments as they come due.

Moreover, when the federal government spends more than it taxes, it is putting money into the economy. Bank reserves are growing, and so are our demand deposits. Remember that: deficits put money into the economy. Taxes take it out. Revenue is burned.

As we discussed, the Fed makes all payments for the US Treasury. When the Treasury cuts a thousand-dollar check – say, it sends a Social Security payment to a retiree – the retiree's bank deposit account is credited by $1000; the bank sends that check on to the Fed for payment. The Fed credits the bank's reserves by $1000.

Usually, the Treasury will then create and sell a US Treasury bond that promises to pay interest. Banks generally prefer to earn higher interest on bonds than they can earn on their reserve accounts at the Fed. As banks buy Treasury bonds, the Fed debits their reserves – banks use their reserves to buy bonds.

Banks are happy to buy the bonds – they are like a savings account that earns more interest than the bank can earn on its reserves. For a bank, buying a Treasury bond is sort of like shifting funds from a checking account at the Fed (reserves) to a savings account at the Treasury (bonds) to earn more interest.

So, what is a US Treasury bond? It is a US government IOU denominated in dollars that promises to pay interest. You can buy them, too! (check out treasurydirect.gov).

Generally, over the course of the year, the Treasury will sell an amount of bonds more or less equal to the amount by which its total spending exceeds total tax revenue – that is, equal to the year's deficit. So, for example, if spending exceeded tax revenue by $1 trillion in 2022, then the US Treasury would create and sell a total of about $1 trillion worth of US Treasury bonds.

Since our nation was founded, the Treasury has run a deficit almost every year, and so it has sold bonds almost every year. What that means is that the total amount of Treasury bonds grows each year. This is often called the government's "debt." Technically, it is only a portion of the total debt because it does not include cash and reserve deposits at the Fed – which are also government IOUs.

But when you hear that the government's debt has reached $30 trillion (in 2022), that is a reference only to the total amount of Treasury bonds issued since the founding of the nation.

That debt is an IOU of the government, but it is an asset of the holder of the bond. It is a "Government owes us"! Keep that in mind.

Back in the late 1990s, after decades of running deficits every year, the US government finally ran a budget surplus. What this means is that the government pulled more tax payments out of the economy than the total of its spending for the year.

YOU DELIVER THE GOVERNMENT'S MONEY ON TAX DAY.

Government was getting out of debt! Hallelujah! Redemption!?!

Remember: people paid their taxes so that government could burn its IOUs.

That should have been a cause for alarm: government burned more currency than it put into the economy!

Or, to look at it the other way round: Americans spent more on taxes than they received from government spending. Uncle Sam was draining our income out of the economy!

And yet media pundits everywhere celebrated the news. President Clinton went on television and announced that his plan was to continue to do this for the next fifteen years! Pull that currency out of the economy and burn it!

President Clinton promised that the entire federal government debt would be retired! Not only would Uncle Sam burn the currency, but he'd also burn all the safest assets in the world – US Treasury bonds.

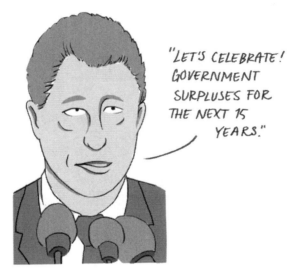

"LET'S CELEBRATE! GOVERNMENT SURPLUSES FOR THE NEXT 15 YEARS."

Let it sink in.

That should have been a national day of mourning. Clinton's plan would impoverish Americans in order to get the government completely out of debt and would continue to run surpluses that would tax us more than government spent – for years and years.

Instead of the government owing us, we'd owe the government! Uncle Sam would drive *us* into poverty.

Of course, Clinton did not see it that way. He thought the government's debt *burdens* America's people. Government is just like a household. The debt must be repaid. Otherwise, poor Uncle Sam will end up in debtor's prison. Taxpayers will have to pay Uncle Sam's bills to bail him out.

These are the scary tales that economists tell around the campfire.

What they forget to tell you is that a government IOU is by definition a "Government owes us." It balances.

Exactly. The government's deficit is our surplus. When government spends more than its "income" (tax revenue), we get to spend less than ours ("save").

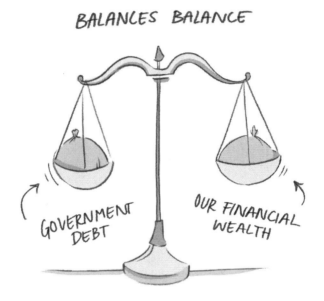

BALANCES BALANCE

GOVERNMENT DEBT

OUR FINANCIAL WEALTH

Uncle Sam's $30 trillion debt (as of early 2022) is his contribution to our financial wealth and health. Thanks, Uncle Sam!

US Treasury debt is safe. There's no chance of default. And Uncle Sam pays interest on it, too! Thanks again, Uncle Sam!

Uncle Sam's budget is nothing like a household's. He is the issuer of the dollar. He cannot run out. You are a user of his currency. You can run out. You have to work for it or borrow it. You cannot manufacture it. That makes a difference.

And, unlike you, Uncle Sam never needs to pay it back (and never will!). He pays interest on his bonds, and when they "come due" (after three months, a year, ten years, or thirty years later) he simply issues other bonds as replacements. If you'd prefer cash, he's got that, too! As well as a long line of potential bond buyers who want the safest asset in the world.

Economists largely understand this – we already quoted a number of them who insist Uncle Sam can always pay all bills due. So why do they try to scare us with campfire tales about insolvency and bankruptcy and hyperinflation?

The famous economist Paul Samuelson once let the cat out of the bag.

He likened the myth that government must balance its budget to the purpose of "old-fashioned religion" that "was to scare people by sometimes what might be regarded as myths into behaving in a way that the long-run civilized life requires."

What he meant was that economists want the fear of a debt monster to get elected representatives to behave themselves – to keep spending low and taxes high. He was afraid that, if they knew the truth, they'd spend like drunken sailors.

In this view of the profession, economists are the high priests of the religion who've got the truth but do not trust you with it.

So, they make up fairytales (government can become insolvent), false analogies (government is like a household), tell scary stories (the USA could become just like Zimbabwe or Venezuela, with sky-high inflation that destroyed their economies), and promote wrong-headed policies (Clinton's plan to run surpluses for fifteen years).

Economist Stephanie Kelton created an aviary classification to identify three approaches to government budget deficits: the hawks, the doves, and the owls.

DEFICIT OWLS UNDERSTAND THAT GOVERNMENT RED INK (DEFICIT) IS OUR BLACK INK (SAVING).

Deficit hawks think government should always balance its budget to avoid the possibility of government default.

Deficit doves are willing to accept temporary government deficits in recessions – when households and firms have reduced spending. Government spending can "stimulate" the economy, replacing lost spending with its own, putting the nation back on a growth path.

However, as the economy recovers, government must cut back (lower spending or raise taxes) to avoid inflation. There should be no tendency for the government's debt to grow over longer time periods.

Deficit owls are the smartest birds. They know that Uncle Sam can never run out of his own money.

They know that "affordability" is never the problem: Uncle Sam can always keystroke the money credits.

They know that government deficits let us save and accumulate financial wealth.

THE AVIARY: HAWKS, DOVES AND OWLS

But they agree that too much spending can be inflationary.

For an owl, the potential constraint on government spending is inflation, not finance.

As Congressman Yarmuth put it: when it comes to funding a government program, the question is not whether we can *afford* it but, rather, can we *resource* it?

If we can find the resources, we can always afford it.

11

Money as Scorekeeping

So far, we've seen that governments can create money by issuing currency and spending it. Central banks can create reserve money by lending and crediting private bank reserve accounts. And private banks can create bank money – demand deposits – as they make loans.

This seems either fantastical or perhaps fraudulent the first time you hear about it. They all just create money out of thin air? They cannot run out? Yes, indeed.

Let's think about money as similar to scorekeeping.

Think about a baseball scoreboard. The score is 21 to 14 in the sixth inning (yes, it has been a hitter's game). The home team scores another run. Where will the scorekeeper get another run to award the home team? Must it be taken away from the visitors?

WHERE'S THE SCOREKEEPER GOING TO FIND ANOTHER RUN?

No, it comes out of "thin air." In the old days, the scorekeeper would look for a card with a five on it to substitute for the four to increase the home team's score to 15. If there were no more "fives," the scorekeeper would have written one on a blank card.

Today, it is all electronic. All it takes is a keystroke to change the 14 up to a 15. Out of thin air.

Scorekeepers cannot run out of runs. You can run out of innings. You can run out of time. You cannot run out of scores.

Note the use of the term "score": as we saw earlier, that term has been passed down to us from the practice of "scoring" a tally stick. Could a seventeenth-century exchequer (treasurer to the king) run out of "scores"? Of course not. All he needed was a knife and a stick.

Banks are our scorekeepers in the game called "the economy" – keeping track of our credits and debits. Today score is kept in electronic entries.

In the old days, you'd bring your passbook to the bank when you made a deposit, and the teller would make an entry and initial it. Today, you log online to watch the ebbs and flows of your bank account: wages are credited, all the payments you make are debited, and the bank keeps score.

With luck, you are "winning" – your score keeps going up.

HOUSEHOLD BALANCE SHEET

KEEPING SCORE AT HOME.

You might also keep track at home on a spreadsheet, recording your assets and liabilities. If you are really organized, you might even plan a budget – showing expected income inflow and spending outgo.

All of this will be denominated in the "money of account" – the US dollar in America; the pound sterling in the UK; and the yen in Japan.

We measure much, almost everything, in money terms.

Guitars, cars, jewelry, dolls. Everything has its price. In the money of account – dollars, pounds, yen, yuan, pesos.

HOW MUCH IS THAT GUITAR?

500 DOLLARS, NOT 500 SONGS

When you go to the grocery store, you see prices also denominated in the money of account – so many dollars for a bottle of cooking oil, so many cents for a pepper. What to buy? So many decisions to make!

You make purchases; the store makes sales – both denominated in dollars. The cash register tallies up what you owe. Your account is debited, the store's account is credited – by the banker who is the scorekeeper.

MONEY EVOLVED AS UNIT
OF ACCOUNT TO MEASURE
MONEY DEBTS

Credit and debt make the world go 'round. We can think of a circle of debits and credits, income and spending. The central bank keeps track of bank credits and debits; banks keep track of household and business credits and debits.

It is all about scorekeeping and settling scores. (There's that word, score, again!)

Today, this is mostly done through keystrokes.

And the scorekeepers cannot run out of them!

12

Rise of the Winners-Take-All Economy

Immediately following World War II, much of what we've learned in this book about government spending was understood by economists and policymakers.

After all, the federal government had grown tremendously – in the 1930s with Roosevelt's New Deal to fight the ravages of the Great Depression, and in the 1940s to fight the fascists.

In World War II, Uncle Sam needed about half of the nation's output to fight the war. Deficits were large and government issued a lot of debt. But it was widely recognized that government could not run out of its own money. And Uncle Sam would not default on the debt.

With the war over, it was time to reduce government's use of resources – so that households and firms could use more. Gradually the economy was transitioned back to peacetime production of goods for household consumption.

Yet, Uncle Sam's share remained at about a quarter of national output – eight times more than in 1929 – and state and local governments also needed their share, too.

BABY BOOMER COMING THROUGH!

Why? Well, the baby baby boomers were a big reason: they needed diapers and schools. Their parents needed houses, highways, bridges, and shopping malls. There was also the Cold War, and then the Vietnam War. And the space race – NASA versus Sputnik. As well as the "war on poverty" fought by Presidents Kennedy and Johnson.

The US economy boomed! Even though the government took a big share, living standards rose significantly – there was plenty left over for households: cars, household appliances, and toys for the kids.

However, growth began to slow in the 1970s, and inflation – meaning rising prices – picked up. This created a strange, new phenomenon: higher unemployment and higher inflation at the same time – called stagflation.

A seismic shift of thinking took hold. Maybe government was too big? Maybe taxes were too high? Maybe government should do less? Maybe government *is* the problem?

REAGAN:

" GOVERNMENT IS THE PROBLEM "

President Reagan ushered in a new era in the 1980s. The solution to the stagflation problem was to cut taxes – especially on the rich. And reduce government spending

– especially spending on the poor. And slash regulations to encourage private initiative. Reducing the role of the government in the economy would restore prosperity, he promised.

This was called supply side economics and was celebrated by a small fringe of economists. It proposed to cut spending on welfare to increase the incentive to work. And promised to balance the government's budget by *reducing* the tax rate – especially for the rich.

This counterintuitive result was called the Laffer Curve: lower tax rates will create so many new jobs and profit opportunities that the economy would boom and tax revenue would rise so quickly that the budget deficit would be eliminated.

The Laffer Curve turned out to be a bit of a laugher: the deficit rose! Oh, never mind, they said. Deficits are not so bad after all.

GET THE GOVERNMENT OFF OUR BACKS!

What really mattered, they said, was to downsize the role of government.

Over the next forty years, this view that a smaller government is better held sway both in Washington and among many economists. They endorsed the notion that the economy does not need so much government guidance. Instead, we can rely on an "invisible hand."

To be sure, this was not completely new – the "father" of economics, Adam Smith, had made reference to it back in 1776. The idea is that the invisible hand of the market is supposed to guide you to make the right choices.

As a consumer, you carefully choose which products to purchase to give you the most satisfaction for the buck. As an employer, you hire just the right number of workers and pay each according to the individual's contribution to production.

THE INVISIBLE HAND
OF THE MARKET

As a student, you choose to study the discipline that will maximize lifetime earnings. And you decide how much of your income you should spend and how much you should save for future consumption.

The market helpfully sends signals to you to help you make the right decisions. What are those signals? Prices! Wages! Interest rates!

Competition is supposed to replace government regulations. Market competition keeps prices low and forces firms to cater to consumers, ensuring high quality and safe products. Employers compete with one another to offer high wages, good benefits, and pleasant working conditions.

DOG-EAT-DOG COMPETITION ENSURES HIGH QUALITY AND LOW PRICES!

President Reagan believed that pursuing your own self-interest would be good for the economy as a whole.

Margaret Thatcher, British prime minister at the time, followed a similar approach, insisting There Is No Alternative (TINA) to free markets.

Indeed, she denied there is any such thing as "society" – there are only individuals, and the duty of individuals is to look out for themselves. They should not look to government to protect them.

By removing government protection, we would stop coddling the poor and provide them with the proper incentive to take responsibility for themselves. Incentivize them to work.

THE RIGHT INCENTIVES GET
THE RAT TO RUN THE MAZE.

Later, President George Bush (the second) declared we were creating the "ownership society" – meaning a society that rewards the true owners. Like President Reagan, he cut taxes on the rich to increase their rewards.

President Clinton followed him and ended welfare "as we know it" – as he put it – substituting time-limited benefits and work requirements – workfare instead of welfare.

He also ushered through nearly complete deregulation of the riskiest part of the financial system – what is called shadow banking. And, as we saw earlier, he promised to end deficits and retire all the federal debt.

These policies unintentionally helped to bring on the worst economic crisis the USA had faced since the 1930s, as the economy fell first into the DotCom bubble of the late 1990s and then the Global Financial Crisis in the 2000s.

That required a $29 trillion bailout of the global financial system, overseen by President Obama and undertaken mostly by the Fed. In addition, Congress allocated about $800 billion for "Main Street" – the businesses and households that make up the rest of the economy.

As we saw earlier, President Obama wanted to spend more but was worried about running out of money.

It took the economy a long decade to recover. President Trump followed President Obama, campaigning on a platform that promised to "Make America Great Again."

MAKE AMERICA GREAT AGAIN!

He gave another tax cut to the rich that he promised would help restore America's greatness. This was another of a long line of tax cuts that can be traced from Reagan to Bush, and finally to Trump.

It was consistent with the view that government needed to be downsized.

But the small government approach was partially to blame for unintentionally leaving the nation ill-prepared for disasters: Hurricanes Katrina, Sandy and Ida (New Orleans, 2005; Eastern USA, 2012; Gulf Coast, 2021), wildfires (Camp Fire, California, 2018), lead in drinking water (Flint, Michigan, continuing), and falling bridges (at least twenty-three have collapsed since 2000).

And then we collapsed into the COVID recession – millions lost their jobs as the pandemic wreaked havoc.

The strange thing is that both recent recessions – the one created by the Global Financial Crisis in 2008 and the pandemic crisis in 2020 – actually increased the share garnered by the very top of the income distribution.

Indeed, they never had it so good. Their income and wealth seem to climb in good times and also climb in bad times.

Heads they win and tails they win, too.

It seems that the long and the short of it is that "getting government off our backs" turned out to benefit the richest. The last four decades have resulted in a tremendous shift of income and wealth toward the top. Income stagnated at the lower end and grew slowly for America's middle class.

The richest country on earth still has approximately 31 million Americans with no health insurance and 35 million who are "food insecure" – meaning they may not know where their next meal will come from.

The COVID pandemic brought home how much inequality had risen since the time of President Reagan. It also exposed weaknesses in our social safety net, including our healthcare system, our provision of childcare for working parents, our system of unemployment benefits, and the supply of housing for low-income families.

Fortunately, both President Trump and his successor, President Biden, swiftly responded with huge relief spending, including sending trillions of dollars' worth of checks to households and businesses.

It seemed policy had taken a different turn – increasing government's role and with greater focus on average Americans.

Is there really an alternative, despite Mrs Thatcher's TINA claim? President Biden announced a "Build Back Better" plan that in many respects seemed to suggest that government would play a bigger role, much as it did in the early postwar period.

Maybe Uncle Sam can afford policy to tackle our multiple challenges?

Let's see in the final chapter.

13

The Way Forward: We Take Care of Our Own

Many have recognized the early post-World War II period as the "Golden Age of Capitalism" – not only for the USA, and not only for the rich countries. Even the lower-income developing countries grew faster than they ever had before or have since.

We were also beginning to tackle issues such as inequality, racism, and discrimination against people of color, women, people with disabilities, and those of alternative sexual orientations. We were making progress on many of those fronts.

But, as discussed in the previous chapter, that began to change in the 1980s as we reduced the role of government in the economy – by reducing regulation but also by tightening government's "purse strings" – and we lost ground.

Why did we do that? A big part of the reason was that there was great fear that government was running out of money and that Uncle Sam's debt would burden us. Government policy was crippled by concern about "where the money will come from."

WE'RE ROASTING THE GOOSE
THAT LAYS THE GOLDEN EGG

What this book has shown is that there is no reason for pessimism. We don't have to roast the goose that lays the golden egg: our government has the sovereign power to spend whatever it takes to get us back on the road to social and economic progress.

In this chapter we are not going to look at particular policies – such as President Biden's "Build Back Better." Instead, we are going to focus on the financing issue: if we can come up with good policies, can we find the money to fund them?

Our hesitancy to spend money to tackle national problems seems to be based on the mistaken belief that finance is a scarce resource. And, indeed, Washington's policy over the past four decades has been focused on deregulating the financial sector on the belief that money is too scarce.

But that is not true: anyone can create money . . . and neither our banks nor our government can run out.

We need to reorient our economy to serving us well – rather than catering to financial markets in the hope that they would somehow carry us out of the doldrums. Our financial system is already too big. We need to focus more on Main Street and less on Wall Street.

OVERSIZED FINANCIAL SECTOR

What can we do turn things around?

First, we must reject the household budget analogy: the government's budget is **nothing** like a household's. Uncle

Sam issues the currency; we use it. Uncle Sam's spending is our income. His deficit is our savings.

Uncle Sam can always afford to help us do our best.

UNCLE SAM CAN ALWAYS AFFORD TO HELP OUT!

Understanding that, all we need is to agree on the policies that would accomplish our goals.

But that won't be easy because we've got to bring Americans together to recognize the benefits of cooperation – what President Roosevelt was able to do the last time our nation faced challenges as serious as those we face now.

It is time to bring the elephants and the donkeys together, united in the desire to get America back on the path to shared prosperity – growth that benefits everyone and that protects the environment.

THE DONKEYS AND ELEPHANTS CAN RESOLVE THEIR DIFFERENCES

We can disagree on many aspects of policymaking: what are the problems we need to resolve; what are the solutions to those problems; what role should government play in implementing those solutions; and so on.

But there is one thing we can agree on: if we have the technical know-how, and if we have the resources, we can always afford to put those resources and know-how to use. That is the reality of our situation: affordability is not the barrier when it comes to government's finances.

Reality is on *our* side. The deficit hawks (and doves) are wrong. Uncle Sam can afford to spend where needed. But we have to match his spending with our resources and use our know-how to get the job done.

We've referred to Professor Minsky several times in this book, and he bears one more quote. He used to always say that "there are as many varieties of capitalism as Heinz has pickles." To be precise: fifty-seven.

Our point in this chapter is that we had a pretty good version of capitalism in the early postwar period. But we have a pretty bad one now. Our current model promotes the idea that greed is good. That it's "every man for himself." That it is a "winner takes all" economy.

Minsky's point was that we can choose another – we do not have to put up with this one.

THERE ARE 57 VARIETIES OF CAPITALISM. LET'S CHOOSE A BETTER ONE.

Let's choose one that recognizes that we are all in this together. We can tackle our problems because we have the money, the resources, and the technology.

We can preserve nature in our parks; we can provide daycare for all children; we can improve our highways and make our bridges safe; we can clean up our rivers and air; we can go to net zero carbon; we can improve subways and trains and extend their reach.

And we can create and improve access to art, music, and positive symbols of our nation's heritage.

We can tackle climate change and better prepare for the next viral outbreak.

All this is within our reach.

As singer Bruce Springsteen put it, "Where's the spirit that'll reign, reign over me; Where's the promise, from sea to shining sea."

"WE TAKE CARE OF OUR OWN"

A MOTTO FOR OUR TIMES

Somewhere along the way, we've lost that spirit. We need to rekindle the promise by pitching in together to take care of one another.

As Bruce Springsteen said, "we take care of our own." "Own" is all of us. All humans. And plants and animals. And our earth.

The great economist John Maynard Keynes – whom we saw before – once said he hoped that economists might someday become as modest and yet as useful as dentists.

AS USEFUL AS DENTISTS

It is a high bar, but maybe this book is a first step. Economists have sometimes misled us with their belief that it is their job to tell "white lies" to scare the population into "behaving themselves."

We think that is the wrong approach. This book trusts you, the reader, with that truth. We trust you to do what you can to spread the truth and to hold policymakers accountable.

The truth is that government faces political constraints. It faces resource constraints. It faces technological constraints.

But it does not, cannot, face financial constraints. Whatever is doable is financially affordable.

Take that idea and run with it.

Index